T0196274

Simon Stargazer III

Simon Sez:

A Glass Half Full, or Half Empty,

Still Has Enough Left for a Drink

James W Haworth
Brings you more thoughts on living life
and having fun doing it, by Simon Stargazer III
(His alter ego)

authorHOUSE®

AuthorHouse™
1663 Liberty Drive
Bloomington, IN 47403
www.authorhouse.com
Phone: 1-800-839-8640

First published by AuthorHouse   12/16/2011

ISBN: 978-1-4685-3102-2 (sc)
ISBN: 978-1-4685-3103-9 (ebk)

Printed in the United States of America

Any people depicted in stock imagery provided by Thinkstock are models, and such images are being used for illustrative purposes only.
Certain stock imagery © Thinkstock.

This book is printed on acid-free paper.

Contents

Chapter One
Aphorisms

Chapter Two
Awareness!

Chapter Three
Disjointed Thoughts

Chapter Four
Famous And Infamous People

Chapter Five
Holiday Thoughts

Chapter Six
How Come I Can't Do That?

Chapter Seven
Nostalgia

Chapter Eight
Shazam!

Chapter Nine
Strange But True

Chapter Ten
Sweet Thoughts

Chapter Eleven
The Way It Should Be . . . Or Maybe It Is!

Chapter Twelve
Things I Wouldn't Say In Public

Chapter Thirteen
Untold Stories I Can't Wait To Read!

First, a tale with one beginning
and three endings.

And then…

Chapter Fourteen
Warm Thoughts

Chapter Fifteen
What Will Be Will Be

Chapter Sixteen
When I Was Young

Chapter Seventeen
Why Would You Do That?

Chapter Eighteen
X-Ray Vision

Chapter Nineteen
You Can't Get There From Here Or Can You?

Chapter Twenty
Zounds

Chapter Twenty-One
More Aphorisms To Tickle Your Brain

Chapter Twenty-Two
Stories to End With

Chapter Twenty-Three
And God Said . . .

Chapter Twenty-Four
I Have A Few Odd Questions, Introductions,
Amorous Thoughts And A Mystery Solved Among
Other Things Of Interest

Credits:

Cover Design:
By James Haworth, Glen Lindahl
And Gary Terrell

Cover background:
Jet in Carina Nebula WFC3 UVIS Full Field

Space Photos Courtesy of:
NASA and the Hubble Space Telescope

Photographic Illustrations:
By James W Haworth

Sketches by James Kimber

Drawings by James W. Haworth

Proof reader: Andrea Reichard

Author photo by Patricia Altman

Forward

My earliest memories in the small town of Woodland California are few and far between. I lived with my mother and grandmother in her big Victorian home. After the second grade, my mother died and I went to live in the Fred Finch Children's Home because my Grandmother was too old and my brothers were too young to take care of me. After the fourth grade my father took me to Reno to live. He had just opened the small Bond Memorial Hospital where he also practiced medicine as an Osteopathic Surgeon.

My life in Reno was short lived, as he died in the middle of my fifth grade year. My uncle and aunt came from Duluth Minnesota to adopt and take me home with them. After my first year in Junior High School, we moved to the St. Louis area. From there, I went to a small Quaker boarding school called Olney, in Barnesville Ohio. After graduation, I attended Earlham College in Richmond Indiana. After earning my degree in Biology, I moved to Indianapolis, where I began work in the medical field at St. Vincent Hospital.

I was fortunate to be in the right place at the right time to get into the field of Ultrasound on the ground floor. Through hard work and the support of the hospital administration, I learned Echocardiography, OB/GYN and Abdominal Ultrasound, as well as Vascular Doppler. This has been my life's work ever since. This background as well as my work with a myriad of patients and medical staff has given me a wealth of experience to base these writings on. My wit and wisdom comes to you from this long and rich heritage.

Dedication

Olney Friends School located in the Appalachian hills of Southeastern Ohio, is an important foundation of the values in my life. There, teachings centered in the gentle ways of Quakerism, helped form my beliefs and outlook on life.

Interaction with classmates from around the world gave me the insight that people are people, no matter where they come from. Each person has an innate goodness that cannot be denied. Throughout High School my roommates were a virtual microcosm of the world, including boys from Mexico, Germany, Egypt and South America, to name a few.

Even after fifty years, it was evident at our class reunion that we have maintained the close nit feelings we had developed during our four years together at this rural boarding school. Better than 90% of Olney's students graduate and become accepted at colleges and universities throughout the country. The quality of her graduates attests to the importance of a small class size and the high teacher to student ratio of 1:4. I'd recommend Olney to any student and parent.

Friends Boarding School, Barnesville, Ohio
www.OlneyFriends.org

Chapter One
Aphorisms

Aphorism
Any
Pithy or
Heavy
Or humorous or
Really
Inspirational
Short saying that
Moves you

A Smile
A
Picture
May be worth
A thousand words

But
A smile
Is contagious

An editorial a day
Won't scare
politicians away!

See expanded version on page 89

BEING
A ONE MAN
TEAM

RARELY
WORKS

*Inspired by a cartoon
on page 101of
The Indispensable
Calvin and Hobbes
By Bill Watterson*

COMMUNICATION
IS LIKE CARPENTRY

Speaking your mind
Is like cutting boards

Measure
Your thoughts twice

Before you utter
Your words

Human Relations
Human relations
Are not always
So human

If this
Describes you
<u>Please get some help</u>!

Introspection

For your
Own protection
Try introspection

Life '09!
Life is what it is . . .
Just try to keep
Up with it!

Grief

The hole in your heart
From grief

Creates more space
For love

Loyalty
Loyalty
Demands
Worthiness!

Old
Even when yer old . . .
Ya still gotta be bold

Old Age
That "I've got to stop
Thinking about things
As I'm on my way
To do other things"
Syndrome

Pulling weeds
Is God's way of
Keeping us Humble

Saint
Someone who
Always had the
Interests of others in mind with
No thought for
Themselves

Singing in the Rain
Titillates the brain

Solitude
If solitude speaks
You better listen

Sorrow
Sorrow
Is a uniquely
Human emotion
Best salved with
The reverence
Of love

No!

Pets
All know
The meaning

It
Means
Wait until
No one's around

(Kids know too)

Thank You!

**Thank you
And
A Smile**

**Is so
Worthwhile**

Time
There
Is never
More nor less than
Everyone needs to get through life

Think about it!

To Find Your Way
To find your way
Each and every day

Let your inner light

Shine through
To guide you

We
Make
Our own
Choices
Regardless
Of other's
Voices

And the results are
Our responsibility!

When used right . . .
Networking power
Can increase with
Use by the hour

Words
Of Wisdom
Are easy to come by

Learning to live by
Them is the
Hard
Part

Your Smile
Your Smile
 Helps other people
 Have a good day.

*(Inspired by Toni at
The Clermont, IN Post
Office)*

Be True

If
You're
True to yourself

You'll
Be true
To Others

It's
Up to us
To make it
Positive

Timely Musings

Time is
On loan from God
It is not ours to keep

Time is
Never lost
It's just misused

Time is to be
Used not abused

Time
Travels
The same
We just use
It with different
Degrees of efficiency

Perspective
should be
Based on reality!

Time is
Time is the constant:
Our ability
To deal with it
Is the variable!

The Gentle Soul

The
Gentle soul
Influences
Without
Fear

Learn
From all
You encounter

Use that knowledge
With care

That Thought

That fleeing
thought
Is rarely caught

Worry

This is
Not to be debated:
Worry is truly overrated

Your Best

Always do your best, I say,
But there's still another day

Life Doesn't Need . . .

Life doesn't need a bookmark
You always know where you are

You Can Only Be Sure Of . . .

You can only be sure of two things in life:

Death and Taxes
But

You can only be late on one.

Happiness

Think and you will find
Happiness is a frame of mind

Failure

Failure learned from
Becomes success!

Getting There

The most important thing
About getting from here to there is
Knowing where there is.

Time Travel

Time travel
Is a one way trip
We all take

Time Goes On

Time goes on
Don't just watch it

Reality

Reality is relative
It changes with time

Any Job

Any job worth doing
Better get done!

Think God!

Think God in all you do
It's really good for you!

*(Inspired by a George
Burns movie)*

Go

Go
With
Serendipity
And see what
Your new life
Just might
Become
Next!

Smiles
Multiply!

An Apple a Day

An apple a day
Works much better when
Eaten with other healthy foods

Speed

Speed kills
Quality
Too!

One Good Turn

One
Good turn
Doesn't get you
Very far in the triptik of life

Pictures

A picture may be worth
A thousand words, but . . .

A conversation about it
Can be very engaging.

A Smile Here

A smile
Here

A smile
There

A smile

E v e r y w h e r e

Pretty soon
The whole
Room is bright!

One Good Turn[2]

One good
turn
Can change
a life

My Favorite Smile

**Belongs to my wife Pat·
And I'll share it with you**

Fly
Fishing
Is another
Of God's ways
To teach patience

Truth

This is what you should do:
To yourself be true

And remember

That little white lie
Follows you till you die

Contagious Things

Smiles
Yawns
Colds
Goodness

Take your pick!

And
Continue
The good work!

If You're Feelin' Blue

If you're feelin' blue
Here's what you do:

Take a trek through the
Corridors of your mind

To see what treasures
You can find

After a while
You'll find a smile

Grab it and give it away
You'll get it back all day

Solitude Explained

Your solitude
May appear rude

But it follows
That it allows

Introspection
Reflection
Detection

Resulting in

Edification
Rumination

And maybe
Education

Something to keep in mind.

The other day I said "How are you?"

She said "Pretty good."

I said, "Well, I'm not pretty,
And I'm not good, but I work
Really hard."

To which she replied:
"Everyone's pretty in some way"

How true it is.

(From a short conversation with Toni Whitehead.)

*And then she wrote: Look inward and see what's
pretty in you and thank God for it . . .*

Questions for Your Inner You

Are you really at peace
In this body you lease?

Does your outer face
Reflect your inner space?

Do you stop playing hero or clown
And take the time to center down?

Do you spend your time wisely then
To hear the still small voice within?

When you've thought this thought
Then do you do what you ought?

Will your conscience be your goad
For when the rubber hits the road?

If you'll do
This for you

You will find
Peace of mind

The Purr Is

Consummate
Contentment

The Purr Explained

A consummate
Source of
Contentment
To all Mankind

Shared with
Abandon by
The Feline
Species

With all
Willing
Recipients

In exchange
For focused
And liberating
Attention

In short:
A stress reducer
For all

Autopilot

More often than not
We're on autopilot

Sometimes it takes a
Jolt to pull us out of it

Tho' we may not be consciously alert
Our brain keeps us from gettin' hurt

This may be OK when things are routine
But in new circumstances keep it keen!

Rain Becomes . . .

To those whose imagination is quite fleet
Rain becomes pixies dancing in the street!

At Day's End

The peace at the end of the day
Should be commiserate with
The stress of the day

If it's not,

You
Need to
Work on it!

It's Spring

Redbud's branches
Of lavender and pink

It's enough to
Make you think:

Let the bells ring!
Wow! It's **Spring!!**

Catfluence!

We have a cat who wanders here and there
With four on the floor and his tail in the air

Often a speedy blur
Shedding balls of fur

He's there to impede
When you try to read

He lets you know if he wants a drink
By standing and meowing in the sink

He sleeps when he wants
After visiting his haunts

But if he sleeps with you at night
This will probably be your plight:

His approach to morning
Is this subtle warning:

Quiet little paws of tactile alarm
Announce morning on your arm

His idea of a snooze alarm
Is some caterwauling charm

And you're fully awake as you fall
After stepping on his fresh hairball!

But all this we endure
Just to hear him purr!

Young at Heart

As our bodies age and grow weary
The child within can remain cheery

Just remember to wake him up
When you get down in your cup

For the spirit remains ever young
And that makes life forever fun!

The Thing About Time

Perception is everything

Time is neither fast nor slow
It took my whole life to get here

The first part seemed quite slow
The last part seemed quite fast.

The difference is perception

What's the best part?
The whole thing!

Fantasy Flight

Enjoy
Your flight
Into fantasy
While you can

Reality lurks
Right behind it!

Fantasy Flight Two

A short flight
Into fantasy is refreshing

An extended flight
May land you in trouble

Round in Square in Round

Breakfast for one, Simon Stargazer III's style.

There are webs, and then . . .

Webs men weave
To deftly deceive

Are a far cry
To my wary eye

From the spider's snare
To catch dinner unaware.

For the one is obscure
And the other is pure.

The spider's intent
Is clearly meant.

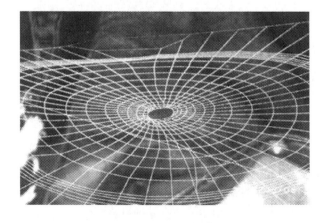

Chapter Three
Disjointed Thoughts

Life is . . .

Life is
A complicated cartoon
Drawn by God for the amusement
Of his angels!

How would you know?

How would you know if you saw a black
Cat on a moonless night at midnight?

That's easy, silly, you'd be out
Walking with a flashlight!

I Think

I think
Therefore, I am . . .
I think . . .

And muttering nary a peep
` I just went back to sleep

Clouds on the Move

The clouds were like
Ships in a battle fleet

In small groups
Lined up so neat

Photograph

A frozen glimpse
Of a nitch in time

The First Sign?

Numbness invades the mind
Leaving my thoughts blind
Would you be so kind
Please help me find
My way in time?

The Cat With Stiletto Toes

I am totally amazed
That she's not phased.

She gets a bit grumpy and all that
But she lets me cut her nails flat

And before I forget, I must mention
The scratching post gets her attention

My color quickly pales
As she works on her nails.

I know she'll soon jump on my shoulder
And those sharp nails will surely hold her

Tons of Steel

All those tons
Of steel afloat

Don't make that
Battleship a boat

Centipede Stampede

A
  Wild
    Centipede
     Stampede
      Would
       Leave
     You
       Lightly
        Trampled
    But
     Not
      Quite
     Crumpled;
     You
       Might
      Say
       Shaken
      But
       Not
        Stirred!

Prison Cookbook:
(*Inspired by Moises Rodriguez*)

Thirteen Ways to prepare Ramen Noodles:
A prisoner's quest for perfect cuisine.

Is an attempt to jump start
A lackluster mealtime routine

A Mime Next Door

Once upon a time
There was a Mime

Who I found would be
A good neighbor to me

He had nothing to say
On each and every day

Lights

I'd think "Good morning, Mime"

Sky light
Sky bright

He'd just reply in kind each time

Carry me thru
All this blue

Till the delight
Of a peaceful night

Then after the night
Of starlight and moonlight

Earth's again alight
With brilliant daylight

Time Traveler

I'm a time traveler
How else did you think
I'd get here?

The Wilderness of the Mind

The wilderness of the mind
Is a lonely place

That's where you put things
You just can't face

They'll come back
To make you blue

And when they do
They'll
haunt You!

Chapter Four
Famous and Infamous People

President Truman

How is it
That a man's Greatness
Can be Summed up so Ineloquently

And yet
At the same time
As succinctly as this?

"The buck stops here."

Mark Twain

He called himself Mark Twin
He could write quite a refrain

A Connecticut Yankee in King Arthur's Court
Has had many a filmmakers' flashy retort

The Adventures of Tom Sawyer, no doubt
Carries the most amount of memory clout

But if I told you another pen name was Josh
You might just think I was full of hogwash!

Samuel Langhorne Clemmens was his name
But Mark Twain was what brought him fame

Elsa

Elegant
Lady
So fitting
As a wife for John

Grandkids

Visiting the grandkids never gets old
Even when they leave you with a cold!

Calvin and Hobbes

Calvin and Hobbes
Had the best jobs

Calvin's was to experience childhood
Hobbes' to make sure it was really good

Calvin was ever so wild and unkempt
He took Hobbes wherever he went

Calvin was so irrepressibly inventive
And Hobbes was equally expressive

Though they were quite extreme
They were the best kind of team

Keeping their imaginations tightly in place
They'd challenge Physics, Time and Space

Till at the end of each adventurous day
Reluctantly exhausted, they'd hit the hay

Heroes

Heroes are
Every day people that
Rise to the
Occasion to
Inevitably
Save the day without a
Moments hesitation

Palindrome

Palin:

First presidential candidate from Alaska*

Drome:
Place where races are held

Palindrome:
Presidential candidate in the race.

Alternatively:

Spelled the same frontward or backward.
Means she's got'cha comin' and goin'!

* Simon's first political prediction!

Riley, Oh Riley . . .

Riley, oh Riley, wherefore art thou?
Quietly conversing with your cow?

Is that where you got your Farm-Rhymes
About those far and distant olden times?

On that distant day, oh so hot
I am certain that you were not

Trying to discover the lost Lewis Carroll
Hiding with Jabberwock in a whisky barrel

Pondering Elizabeth Barrett Browning
With quiet romantic thoughts burning?

Or perhaps peering into a future's haze
Of some of Ogden Nash's poetic maze

For you are the down to earth
Poetry's 20th century rebirth

Written in memory of James Whitcomb Riley
The revered "Hoosier Poet"

The Name Dropper

Name dropping's a way of life
Frequently fraught with strife

For those living vicariously
For the glow of camaraderie!

Volunteers:

Volunteers are the
Ones who cares about others
Leaving the comfort of their home
Under all sorts of conditions with
No thought for the time it takes.
This person
Exudes
Excellence in attitude with
Respect for others

Thank you for being one, if you are.
If you're not, then thank one for me.

Wisdom

It doesn't
take a
sage

To know

Wisdom
comes with age.

Inspired by Ned C Boatright

Rosy Toes

When you've got rosy toes
The color of a drunk's nose

Everyone knows
Where you goes

I'll tell you why:
Dr. Schlichter's the guy!

He's the go-getter
Who makes it all better!

Inspired by a trip to my podiatrist
(and, yes, that's him above!)

Lewis Carroll Revisited

(What the Walrus Said, In Reality)

The time has come, the Walrus said . . .
(The first thing that came into his head)

But then he stopped and closed his eyes
While considering how to get rid of his flies

Then he quietly drifted off to sleep
And we never heard another peep!

(I couldn't resist roasting Mr. Carroll's work!)

Tribute to a Gal Named Liz . . .

There once was a gal named Liz.
A wonderfully talented Echo wiz

She had an epiphany when Kathy quit
And felt she could make Echo more fit

She took her new job with gusto and spirit
Determined to make a grand run of it

Off on the run to management class
Went this determined young lass

She worked as hard as she could . . .
Much harder than splitting wood

Accreditation was such a chore
It made two years feel like four

And if that wasn't bad, she was blessed
By steering us through going paperless

This while doing the budget and AHN Echos
How she had the energy only Heaven knows

She worked so hard to make everything right
That it took her all just to stay in the fight

Then finally she realized the toll it was taking
It was her family that she was truly forsaking

And step down holding back the forming tears
To be mother in your family's important years.

For what you've done, you should be proud
And we welcome you back into the crowd

Thanks for a job well done. The Echo Techs.

Written for Liz Murray of The Care Group, 2008)

The Hoosier Salon

Visit the Hoosier Salon
Where artists get it on!

(Our Hoosiers venting
With artistic rending)

Written for Willa Bowen Van Brunt

Your Honey

When You're Feeling blue
And you don't know what to do

Go see your honey
She'll make it sunny!

Her smile so true
Will uplift you

For she's a major part
Of your inner heart

A Tribute to Edgar Alan Poe

It was a dark and foggy night
Complete with surrealistic light

Slinky shapes were oozing all around
Hovering ever so closely above ground

Approaching moans whispered eerily
As I hurried through the night stealthily

Turning the next corner, I came face to face
With a bright door and quickly entered my place

I was finally away from the dark and foggy night
Where I'd just about died from fright!

Golden Gate Park photo by Mila Zinkova

Marylee Lear
Volunteer Extraordinaire

She pleasured us with her presence

God put her where she was
For his own reasons . . .

To learn, teach and help others
Till He was satisfied.

And He is.

So His good and faithful servant
Was brought to Him

We will remember and miss her
Every day

**In Case You Don't Have any . . .
This is What my Grandkids look like:**

And this is how long you'll love them!

To

**Memories
Are made special
By the people in them**

**Snow
Is God's
Way of telling
Us that those pesky
Mosquitoes are gone!**

Chapter Five
Holiday Thoughts

Christmas Eve

Christmas Eve comes but once a year
The day before the Lord came here

The day that work slows down
So folks can get out of town

Then we each celebrate the gift He gave . . .
The one God meant for our lives to save.

Christmas Day

Instill
If you will

In the minds of the young
Why what is done, is done

Teach them the reason
For the season

And it matters not
Which religion you've got

For there is no greater love
Than that which is given from above

The Day After Christmas

Christmas Eve has come and gone
And so has Christmas day

Now that that's all done,
I have something to say

It's not how big a pot you've got
Or whether you're rich or poor

It's not about all the presents you got
This holiday's about so much more

Did you give thanks to the Lord above
For all the family and friends you love

And did you thank him for the life you live
And are there those that you need to forgive?

New Year's Timely Thoughts

A watched pot never boils
A watched clock slows down
Lonely nights linger longer
The New Year starts at midnight

Though the spark of love quickens the heart
It has been proven that . . . Lovers live longer!

So . . . May your New Year be loverly!

The Snows of Fall

The blowing snows of Fall
Are the most colorful of all

Large flakes of red and yellow
Drift through air oh so mellow

Thickly covering the grass so green
Arriving just in time for Halloween

The 4th of July

It was the 4th of July in 1776
America had just put in the fix

The war against England was won!
It was liberty and freedom for everyone!

The Declaration of Independence had been signed
And we found it would last and last, just as designed

Long may it stand
Across this great land

As one nation, under God
With liberty and justice for all

Black, white, yellow, brown or red
We believe in all for one and one for all

Snow
Surely
No one
Objects to a
White Christmas!

Holiday Fatigue

Holiday fatigue is your due
If you wrap presents till you're blue

Next year start before Thanksgiving
And life will be more worth living!

The Snow-nayers

The morning after
Christmas
The ground was quite
white

I'm glad it waited till
Late Christmas night!

Speaking of Thanksgiving

Give thanks every day that you live
And don't limit to family when you give

And when you give, give direct
Make it to some who don't expect

Chapter Six
How Come I Can't Do That?

Please Let Me Go!

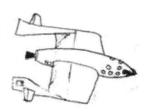

C'mon Burt Rutan
Let me in that can

You so lovingly call Spaceship One
Take me to space before were done

"Sure, by all means", Burt hollars
"But first give me a million dollars"

The Reality Show of Life:

You
say you
Just got
married?

Don't look now,
but
The rules
just changed

And
The in-laws
Don't play by
Them either!

A Day at the Fair

A day at the fair is such a treat
But oh! How it kills my feet!

When I finally hobble back home
I vow never again at the fair, I'll roam

Crickets Are Good Luck

Crickets are lucky, you say?
Just try to catch one today!

Their jumper is automated
Your quick lunge is ill fated.

They have a fabulous knack
For not being where they're
at

And finally you moan . . .
Their luck is their own!

Chapter Seven
Nostalgia

When I Was Ten

This memory was special when I was ten
My mom made fried chicken out of a hen!

I was glad, 'cause what the heck
I was the one she used to peck!

The Olney Life

Life at Olney's Sandy Ridge
Is a multi-national privilege
In an expansive, yet miniature scale
In the middle of Ohio's hill and dale

Where that still small voice
Is heard quiet and clear
With an impact that
Reaches both far and near

It changes the lives forever more
Of all who enter and leave her door
Both students and staff will attest
This experience is one of the best

*Inspired by my experiences at Olney Friends School
In Barnesville, Ohio where I attended High School
And lived on campus for four years.*

The Kite That Wouldn't Fly

Once a year our school had a day
Kind of special, or so they say

Build a kite and put it in the air
Out on the prairie, windy and fair

This went on for years, quite unabated
Some kids loved it, for some it was hated

It was a challenge for my Dad and I,
Father and son, building a kite to fly

Unfortunately, when he made his bid
My Dad forgot that he was not a kid.

Hardwood trim and wrapping paper
Were destined to fail in this caper.

We worked hard and finished with pride
A box kite with heavy paper on each side.

At the field there were kites all around
Brightly waiting to get off the ground

We had a winner, we just knew
But like a rock was how it flew!

And now my story is quite done
For me and my Dad it was still fun

*This was 1950 Reno, Nevada, before I
even thought about gambling and slots.*

My first Plane Ride!

Are you old enough to remember when
The old DC-3 was propeller driven?

It had a motor mounted on each wing
World War II troops flew in that thing

Well, in 1948 when I was seven
I thought I came close to heaven

We took off out of San Francisco
In a long sweeping turn, really low,

Out over the ocean, it was really neat
I saw the ocean waves almost at my feet

I had a great view, as you can imagine
Seated behind the right wing and its engine

I got an eyeful, and that's no joke,
When it belched fire and smoke!

The pilot came on the intercom
And said "Everyone be calm"

"I got the fire put out
And we'll turn about"

When we landed again we were met by mechanics
And twenty minutes later, by golly, it was fixed.

The stewardess gave me my wings and said let's go!
We're not gonna stop till we get to Reno!

Chapter Eight
Shazam!

System Crash

A system crash is like
A thief in the night

It robs you and leaves
You in such a plight

How can you know
What you've got

If you've never
Inventoried the lot

So, before you shut down
Just back up your files

And if it crashes
You'll be all smiles!

Hand Sanitizers
The Hand of God
Is the ultimate
Sanitizer

Night Patrol

The night is warm
The air is so dry

It's a perfect time
For the bats to fly

Cleaning the night air
Of bugs everywhere!

Night after night
They keep up the fight

But don't you fear
They won't come near

New house priority #1

That bedroom curtain
Gotta get up for certain

For it'd be quite rude
For you to see us nude!

White!

It'll be white
By tonight!

I guess I was right
About the white!

Now I can't wait for the sheen
Of new mown grass's green!

*(Written after snow blowing 12 inches off
my driveway!)*

The Presidential Pants

Now that he's become the President Elect
He's got new baggage he may soon regret!

He'll be paying long time dues
For those brand new IOUs!

Like many Presidents from the past
He'll find his puppet strings at last

The support that helped him grab the brass ring
Will temper him with that golden puppet string

How will he bring the change for which we asked
If he's already enlisting politicians from the past?

And so it goes:
Political throes

Winter over takes summer
For some that's a bummer

But the good news is great
The years are limited to eight

And if we don't like'em any more
We get to vote'em out in four!

And give some one else a chance
To put on the Presidential pants!

And now I reiterate to you all out there
All Presidents need everyone's prayer

*(I have observed that Presidents, present
and past, find that their views and actions are
irresistibly affected by the office and the
diverse forces that the world brings to bear on them.)*

Fear at Midnight

Makes you want to flee
Ever so quickly
And quietly
NOW

Redeeming Quality

Every day
Has a redeeming quality

It may
Only matter just to me

But it's there
Whether I find it or not

I don't always
Put the right key in the slot

But look
For it I must

Or my
Mind might rust

Don't Mess With the Cat!

Purkinje
(my cat)

Chapter Nine
Strange But True

Cat School

I learn so much from my cat

Like how great it is to have
Fingers and a wash cloth

So I don't have to wash
My face quite like that

Picture this

Yacht Club Harbor:
(With sailboats galore)

A bunch of dead trees
Reaching out of the
Water to the sky!

Cemetery

Marble orchard with
Mixed varieties
And sealed roots

Jail Time

When one is in jail
Time flies like a snail

Every 5 years

When I was 5, I was sick
When I was 10, in love and every day was forever
When I was 15, I was invincible evermore
When I was 20, I was a student in love
When I was 25, work and love; push came to shove
When I was 30, I had a kid of one to love
When I was 35, another of two, more to love
When I was 40, a position of more responsibility
When I was 45, it was more work a and new love
When I was 50, work was too much and I was gone
When I was 55, I was movin' on with a new job
When I was 60, I got a job at a better place
When I was 65, Almost ready to quit the race
When I was 68, I said: "I hope I'm outta here, so I can join my dear!" But Wall Street kicked my rear!
When I'm 70, I plan to be retired for than a year!

So, tell me . . . what have your "5's" been like?

Snow and Ice

Some say snow & ice
Should be kept in its place
Quite far from the human race

They'd be at odds with us
Who would rather ski
Than take the bus

Twins

There are twins
And then . . . well,
There are twins!

Keep this under your hat
Did you know that . . .

At TCG* we have a bunch of twins(!?)

Two are identical, to boot
Now ain't that a hoot?

Enter, if you will,

Temeka and twin Sharmeka
Followed by, if you will,
Nakia and twin Nakisha

That means twice the smiles
And double the wiley wiles!

Temeka and Nakia work in adjacent pods
At The Care Group, Cardiology
(but their twins don't work there)

Ashes to Ashes

Ashes to ashes and dust to dust
It makes me glad that we won't rust

As I've Grown Older . . .

As I've grown older
I have found that my class
Of acquaintances has improved

I now know quite a few more
Doctors, Podiatrists, Dermatologists
Nurses and other medical practitioners!

Children

**Children
Are the teachers
Of patience!**

Cool Bunny

Chapter Ten
Sweet Thoughts

The Mourning Dove

Cooing of the Mourning Dove:
An early morning sound I love.

Young Love

Love's early phase
With it's adoring gaze

I'd Trade my Ring . . .

You say the job's got a perk?
Well, I've got quite a quirk

Here's my deal:
End every meal

With the best
Of the West

That would be a Twin Bing
At the end of the dining.

Written for Lori Pierce, who loves 'em

*(if you're not from Iowa or the Dakotas,
you wouldn't know about Twin Bings . . .)*

The Circle of Your Life

You find you're in a cocoon
A wonderfully warm womb

Soon your world
Becomes unfurled

All of a sudden it's bright and shiny
And you get really teary and whiney

You graduate to a small cage
In this, your first year of age

Then as you get a bit older
Mom and Dad get bolder

Now you're given quite a lot
Of freedom to venture about

A bit later you're done with school
And go for the gold is now the rule

The world is your oyster
To travel and explore

You find a mate and settle down
The circle starts to come around

When kids start coming out
You relearn what life's about

Before you know it you retire
Enjoying life seated by the fire

Finally the illnesses of old age
Make your bed your last cage

As you make your final peace
And give your body its release

You join God in the warmness above
Where everything's full of light and love

Serenity

In the quiet
At the end of the day . . .

Serenity reigns

Luxuriate in it to . . .
Ease your pains

My Belle

My Belle
So swell!

With a heart of gold
Or so I've been told

She's such a gentle soul
Who likes to romp and roll

And when it's dress up time
She doesn't seem to mind

Black from head to toe
She's a great dog to know

Like a turtle dove
She's easy to love

My Belle
So Swell

Written for Chris and Christie and their dog Belle,
who died from bone cancer this summer.
(see the lump on her leg . . . it got lots bigger)

Chapter Eleven
The Way it Should be . . . or Maybe it is!

Ah! This is the Life!

We share a bit of our life with you
You know . . . this is what we all do

We do what you can't do for your self
This is the real sharing of the wealth!

Whether it's doctor, tech, MA, clerk or nurse
This sharing comes from our life's own purse

And you know the best part?
It comes straight from the heart

Now get out there and share the real wealth!

Written for everyone in health care.

Change We Can Count On

A perfect inspiration
Can change the nation

But one man can't do it all
Many must follow the call!

But first we must study the inspiration
To see if it's right for the whole nation

Choice

Regardless
Of how the world
Treats you

You still
Have a choice

And a
Responsibility

From the Lowliest . . .

From the lowliest to the Prez
This is what Simon Sez:

Ya gotta treat'em right
From mornin' till night!

Commercials
Purveyors of what-not
That you wish you'd got
Or maybe not!

If We Would . . .

If, the gifts within,
We would <u>all</u> share

The world would
Be better <u>everywhere!</u>

Greatness

Greatness
Comes when
Actions speak
Louder than
Words.

America
Took action
Tuesday, 11-4-08

The
Greatness
Will come when
We all pitch in
To make it
Happen

Thank you

Thank you
And a smile

Is so very
Worthwhile!

Inspired by Audrey, receptionist at the Care Group

No Matter . . .

No matter who impedes
An American succeeds!

Days

Father's day
Mother's day
Kid's day

We
Should
Celebrate
Each day
For
What it is:
A gift from God

Message to the Nations of the World

Be Green
Not Mean!

Life May Not Be Fair . . .

Life may not be fair
But you can make it better

There are Always New Arrivals . . .

Sometimes I shop at Tuesday Mornings.
The message on their plastic bags is:
There are always new arrivals . . .

That gave me pause . . .

That is what life is all about.

Sometimes it is a new place we arrive at . . .

    In our thoughts
    A physical destination
    A spiritual insight
    Other (you fill in the blank)

Sometimes it is something that arrives for us . . .
Unexpectedly . . . mail, on the radio or on TV

    A person we are introduced to
    A challenge to our personal, work or social life
    A new patient, a new job, or a new concept

The bottom line:

    It is the new arrivals that make up our life,
    so use them the best you can to help define it.

Oh . . . . and don't forget, God is responsible
for delivering them, so keep that in mind too.

Plan

Better think things through
Before you do what you do

Stocks

If you're going to deal in stocks
Consider this before you pull the chocks

Life is the most important commodity
Not steel, oil, corn, beef . . . or tea!

The 14th

I say
The 14th
Should be
Valentines Day
Every month

We need more
Love in the
World!

The Dental Experience

The dentist drill's whir
May cause quite a stir

But when it's used right
The result's a real delight

The Veteran

I worked on a vet the other day
He fought in a war far away

I thanked him for what he'd done*
He said he wouldn't have done it for just anyone

But he'd do it again for our country
So it would stay free for you and me

I hope you thank all the vets you meet

Thoughtful Giving

Solicitations
For Donations

Fill all your mail
Like rain and hail

(So please be very discerning
Spending what you're earning)

Value

Value is
Almost Always higher with
Less errors when work
Is Under pleasing
Good Environmental conditions

Alternatively:

The Value of a product is
Almost always
Less when the work is
Done Under
Extreme duress

Water

Widely known as the elixir of life
It's often the cause of national strife

The universal solvent, chemically,
Drinking fountains give it away free

Some people buy it by the bottle
Priced by the ounce, expensively!

A word from the Muse:
Refill that bottle you use!

Chapter Twelve
Things I wouldn't Say in Public

An Editorial a Day Expanded

An editorial a day
Won't scare politicians away!

It doesn't give them a fright
They love the limelight!

They rely on the fact
They'll still be voted back!

For voters memories are short
They'll have forgotten a bad report

Blind Loyalty

Is practiced only by dogs
And the ignorant public

Eventually even dogs
Will learn from it.

Life's a Cartoon

Life's a cartoon . . .
Drawn by God
For the amusement
Of his angels

Ignorance is bliss

I'd be remiss
If I ignored this

Ignorance has a big flaw
When it comes to the law

Just 'cause you don't know the way
Doesn't mean you won't have to pay

The State of the Media

In utmost truth
If I were uncouth

I would write this verse
To avoid uttering a curse:

The media's not doing so well
In fact, to avoid noticing the smell

When I take the paper out of its wrapper
I wait until I'm firmly seated on the crapper!

(Inspired by comments from my brother Thayer and apparently shared by brother-in law Bill in Las Vegas!)

Venting

Venting is an
Exceptionally important,
Non-violent, Stress relieving,
Technique, important to survival

(Especially when practiced in private!)

If You . . .

If you stop getting old
You start getting cold

Life's Funny . . .

Life's funny till
You stop laughing.

When you stop laughing
God says "Come visit Mr. Hope."

You have to be old enough to
Remember Bob Hope to appreciate
The strength of his humor.

Parkinson's Disease

Parkinson's disease
Is low level exercise
Without the effort!

*Do you suppose the
Heart rate increases?*

Autism

I think I oughta do this
So I will . . .

I gotta do this
So I will . . .

Gotta do this
So I will . . .

Gotta do this . . .

<u>Don't bother me!!</u>

I'm doing my routine . . .

Doing my routine . . .

My routine . . .

Everyone Drops Dead . . .

The doctor's job
Is to prolong
The timing

Chapter Thirteen
Untold Stories I Can't Wait To Read!

The Darkness Before the Dawn

It was 6:00 AM as Adam wandered down the street in a daze. The twilight was less than gleaming as he strode through the murky mist toward the river. He caught the reflection of eyes between trash cans. "I wonder what that was" he grumbled in a low gravelly voice, hoping that it was just a cat rather than the legendary fat rats that resided in the area.

His shift as the night watchman at Wellerman's warehouse had been less than stellar. He was heading to the Sunrise Dinner for a cup of Java, a couple of eggs, bacon and toast on his way home. He had an unsettled feeling as, out of the corner of his eye, he sensed, rather than saw a shadowy form darting between the trees. Adam quickened his steps as he approached the diner, but he never reached the door.

Before he could react, Adam was flat on his back and being dragged between the buildings. At 290 pounds whoever was doing the dragging must have been huge, but when Adam managed to turn his head enough to look, he was flabbergasted at what he saw. The shadowy figure was thin and couldn't have weighed more than 140 pounds. Furthermore, he wasn't even breathing hard. Then it struck him . . . He was lying on a wheeled cart, six inches off the ground! When he tried to move his arms it was as though he was encased in thick gel. With great effort he was able to slowly raise his arm about a foot, but to no avail. Despite the attempt, his arm was inexorably drawn back to his side. He was fastened down with numerous bungee cords.

As he puzzled over what had happened, he realized that as they were moving forward, light traveled with them, driving away the shadows of the surrounding buildings. Where was it coming from? If he turned his head just enough, he could see the shimmering bright surface that he was lying on. That was what was illuminating their surroundings. As they traveled on in this manner, Adam thought the light was fading. It wasn't.

When Adam awoke he found himself in a windowless room, with a ceiling no more than six feet high, and he could tell that the room was moving, though he had no idea how fast. The room was tilted about ten degrees down. One wall was curved gently from floor to ceiling. Though he could not see the outside, he could feel the gentle rise and fall of the room over time. Was he in some sort of submarine? Where could they be headed?

The room was well lit, and equipped with a bed, where he was lying, a chair and desk with work light. There were three doors on the non-curved walls. One door was locked. The second door revealed a closet with an assortment of clothes, which appeared to be in his size. It was then that Adam realized that his clothes had been removed, and he was clad only in the equivalent of a hospital gown. He picked out some underwear, shoes and socks, a maroon shirt and khaki pants. The room had no mirror, but he felt that he was more or less presentable . . . not that he cared. He was more interested in figuring out what was going on.

He checked out the last door and found, as he had hoped, that it was indeed a bathroom, complete with shower. Thirty minutes later, Adam felt much better.

After thoroughly checking out every inch of the walls in the two rooms, he sat down to check out the contents of the desk drawers. Nothing surprising . . . just what one might find in a hotel room . . . with one exception. As he ran his hand along the surface of the desk, part of the surface became a view screen accompanied by a virtual keyboard and finger pad with its associated cursor on the view screen. There were several icons on the screen with annotations in some type of language that he could not recognize. They appeared to be a combination of Chinese pictograms that merged with Egyptian Hieroglyphics. Intuitively, he clicked on one of the icons. Instantly, the view screen became what appeared to be a radar or Doppler topographical mapping of the terrain they were traversing.

Confirming his assumption that he was in a submarine, Adam could make out moving forms of various sizes, which he assumed were different types of fish, dolphins, sharks and the occasional whale. Just as Adam was beginning to see what appeared to be large buildings in the distance, the screen disappeared and he was sitting at what seemed to be a writing desk again. The room lights gradually dimmed out and he began to feel really strange.

When he awoke, Adam realized the room was no longer moving. He wasn't in the same room, nor was he himself.

Once again, he was in a hospital type gown. It didn't take him long to realize that some serious changes had been made in his body. His fingers and toes were now quite elongated. His skin had a blue/black sheen to it, and when he ran his hand through his hair, it wasn't there. And yes, you guessed it, he had row upon row of what appeared to be gills on either

side of his neck, which was also much thicker than before. He threw off the gown and continued his self evaluation. He was much slimmer and his skin had a roughness along his back, but was smooth on his chest and abdomen.

Further evaluation of his head revealed that his eyes now appeared to be more than two inches in diameter, and his nose was just a flattened protuberance with multiple small nostrils in four vertical rows. He now was half fish! Adam flexed his fingers and toes and realized that with concentration, he could extend webbing up to the fingertips and to the tips of his toes, creating perfect paddles. The same concentration also produced a finlike extension from his spine. "Looks like I'm not in Kansas anymore" he said in what now was a rather wispy soft voice.

"You're right, Adam, you're absolutely right. Welcome to New Atlantis." said a sonorous and yet soft voice. Adam looked up from his self evaluation. The speaker's body was similar, but obviously female. "Where is this New Atlantis? What am I doing here? How did you do this, and why?"

"My name is Aquarine. I and many of my fellows have rescued you and a few thousand others from the surface of our world. Your world on the surface is embroiled in a conflict that began in the Middle East and has escalated into total nuclear war. This is the third time in our planet's history that man's development of nuclear capabilities has come to this. The first time, we Atlantians saw what was coming and were able to build a dome over our island. We subsequently were able to use powerful lasers to separate our island from the seafloor and seal it off as well. Using our advanced technology, we were able to drive our island

like a submarine. We found a place on the ocean bottom that would be safe from the radiation that was destroying the surface. Thousands of years later, we were able to return selected couples to the surface to begin over.

Once again humankind became evil and depraved beyond hope of redemption. God directed a man you call Noah, to build an arc in order to save a few representatives of the earths inhabitants. In order to protect us, He instructed that it was to be called an arc. In reality, it is a gigantic submarine. As you may have guessed, it is still in use today. That may explain why no one has been able to find it on Mount Ararat. Oh, and by the way, Noah did live for more than 900 years, as we also have. He is my great, great, great grandfather. And he is the captain of this great submarine.

Here on Atlantis, you will find that your life will be greatly extended. And when the time comes that the earth is once again free of radiation, you and your children and grand—children will return to the surface to rebuild it once again.

Hopefully this time, by our judicious selections, we will have eliminated the genes of future discontent. Oh, and one more thing", she said. "Global warming is cyclic, just as some of your scientists thought. But it's not due to greenhouse gasses . . . it's due to the build up of nuclear radiation."

In a soft and compassionate voice, she said: "My advice this time is to use natural energy sources of power."

And thus began the second long darkness before the dawn of a new civilization.

From The Darkness . . . Illumination! (Version two)

It was 6:00 AM as Adam wandered down the street in a daze. The twilight was less than gleaming as he strode through the murky mist toward the river. He caught the reflection of eyes between trash cans. "I wonder what that was" he grumbled in a low gravelly voice, hoping that it was just a cat rather than the legendary fat rats that resided in the area.

His shift as the night watchman at Wellerman's warehouse had been less than stellar. He was heading to the Sunrise Dinner for a cup of Java, a couple of eggs and toast on his way home. He had an unsettled feeling as, out of the corner of his eye, he sensed, rather than saw a shadowy form darting between the trees. Adam quickened his steps as he approached the diner, but he never reached the door.

Before he could react, Adam was flat on his back and being dragged between the buildings. At 290 pounds whoever was doing the dragging must have been huge, but when Adam managed to turn his head enough to look, he was flabbergasted at what he saw. The shadowy figure couldn't have been more than three feet tall, and wasn't even breathing hard. Then it struck him like a Mack truck . . . He was floating about six inches off the ground! When he tried to move his arms it was as though he was encased in thick gel. With great effort he was able to slowly raise his arm about a foot, but to no avail. Despite the attempt, his arm was inexorably drawn back to his side.

As he puzzled over what had happened, he realized that as they were moving forward, light traveled with them, driving away the shadows of the surrounding buildings. Where was it coming from? If he turned his head just enough, he could

see the shimmering bright surface that he was lying on. That was what was illuminating their surroundings. As they traveled on in this manner, Adam thought the light was fading. It wasn't.

When Adam awoke he found himself in a windowless room, with a ceiling no more than five feet high, and he could tell that the room was moving, and fast at that. Though he could not see the outside, he could feel the gentle rise and fall of the room over time. He was able to move again, though it was somehow strange. Then he realized that it was as if he only weighed about a third of his normal weight and he had to use care not to bounce into the ceiling as he moved.

There appeared to be no specific point of illumination. Light seemed to emanate from every surface with a soft glow. When he reached out and touched the wall, an area about three feet in diameter became instantly transparent, allowing him to see what appeared to be stars rapidly moving past on the other side of the wall. When he took his hand away, the wall appeared to be solid again. But if he slid his hand along the wall, the transparent area moved with it.

Adam found that by experimenting he could double tap on the wall and keep the area of transparency stable when he moved away. He moved around the room continuing to exercise his newly discovered ability and soon had converted most of the circular wall into windows. He could see outside, all around his room and realized that he was indeed traveling through space at an incomprehensible speed.

Before Adam could complete exploring his new environment, the walls slowly became opaque, and the luminosity of the

walls decreased until he was in total darkness. Though he could not discern why, he slowly began to lose consciousness. Before he blacked out, he felt a gentle probing along his arms, legs and torso.

When Adam awoke the room was again bathed in total bright light and he found himself surrounded by a myriad of small beings. He felt no fear, and in fact there was a distinct aura of pleasurable peace in the room.

As he looked around, studying his hosts, he observed that they were humanoid in appearance, with inch thick peach colored fuzz covering their bodies. They wore no clothes, other than a covering on their fore-arms, which appeared to have buttons, dials and view screens. Their feet had four toes in the front and two at the heel. Their hands had four fingers and two opposing thumbs, one of which appeared to be much longer than the other, and was totally flexible. It was readily apparent that there were both males and females.

Their eyes were very large, and to his surprise, numbered eight, positioned two in front, two on each side and two in the back of the head, and one on the end of each elongated thumb. Perfect for exploring inside of things, Adam thought.

Having made this observation, Adam suddenly realized that he no longer was wearing his clothes. There was, however, a gel type substance covering of his mid section, which was slowly receding. There were what appeared to be tiny, totally healed, scars all over his body. Hmmm! How long had he been out? Almost as soon as he completed the thought, he heard a vast chorus speaking as one, in his mind, which said: "Seven days and nights of your time". Peach furs nodded their heads in unison, with warm smiles.

We have repaired many inconsistencies with your internal systems, which will improve both your longevity and your efficiency. Additionally we have unblocked many of the pathways in your brain which have been in place for many of your generations. We have been sent by the God of the Cosmos. He has ascertained that your kind has finally evolved to this pre-determined point in His Plan for humanity.

Welcome to our plane of existence. We are now at the center of what you call the Big Bang, where it all started. You are in the Heart of God. You will be joined by several thousand of your fellows in the next few hours. In the meantime, you will experience a continuing transformation, required for your new life's work implementing His final plan. When it is complete, you will truly know what it means to be "Made in the image of God". Your life's work and how it will be done will become clear to you. As Adam pondered this last thought, he slowly became aware of thousands of new minds joining with his.

You, the chosen, will begin your work tomorrow, on the date given to your Mayan ancestors. This date, which the world has long awaited and feared, is known to you as 12/12/12.

And now, here is the final version, which is written for Adrienne, who likes romantic novellas.

Darkness to Intrigue

It was 6:00 AM as Adam wandered down the street in a daze. Twilight was still distant as he strode through the murky mist

toward the river. He caught the reflection of eyes between trash cans. "I wonder what that was" he grumbled in a low gravelly voice, hoping that it was just a cat rather than the legendary fat rats that resided in the area.

His shift as the night watchman at Wellerman's warehouse had been less than stellar. But it afforded him the luxury of time to think uninterrupted. He was heading to the Sunrise Dinner for a cup of Java, a couple of eggs, oatmeal and toast before driving home. He had an unsettled feeling as, out of the corner of his eye, he sensed, rather than saw a shadowy form darting between the trees. Adam quickened his steps as he approached the diner, but he never reached the door.

A beautiful statuesque woman came out of nowhere and threw her arms around his neck. "Come wiz me to zee Casbah!" she said in a low throaty whisper in his ear. Adam grinned ear to ear. "Angie, knock off the fake accent! Where you been, girl? I haven't heard from you in over a month. I thought maybe you left town or something."

"I had to lay low for a while. One of my old classmates, Ray, is in town and has been looking for me. You remember Ray, don't you?" Adam gave her a funny look. "You mean that gawky tall skinny guy that kept following you around like a lovesick puppy?" Angie rolled her eyes and said "You got it!

Only now he's built like one of those big Saturday night wrestlers. Adam, you gotta help me! He may look great now, but he still gives me the creeps.

But hey! You big lunk, kiss me like you mean it! I could hardly wait to get back to you and your strong arms." Adam was quick to comply and slow to come up for air. Then he got serious. "Look, I'll take you up to my place, you'll be safe there for a while . . . he doesn't know I live here. You can fix me the breakfast I'm missing while you catch me up on what else has been going on." She grinned and said: "That's not all I'm gonna fix for you, Darlin'!"

Taking advantage of the darkness, they walked back to where Adam had parked his car. Being somewhat of a health nut, he always parked near the diner and then walked the half mile to his job at Wallermans.

Once in his car, Angie melted once more comfortably into his arms. "It's so good to be back, Adam. It was all I could do to stay away long enough to ditch Ray." After another steamy kiss, Adam started the car and they drove to his home farther up the river. His house was located about a quarter mile off the road on a quiet cove surrounded by trees with lush undergrowth. His entry road was more like a tunnel. The branches of the massive oak and maple trees on either side met above the road and blotted out the starry night sky.

The road stopped at the edge of a cliff overlooking the river.

Adam pushed a button on the dash and their car began to descend into a shaft the width of three cars. Once they were about twenty feet down, a massive panel slid noiselessly over them, sealing the shaft above. The darkness slowly dissipated

as they continued their journey down. Some three hundred feet down, the elevator stopped. A panel in the wall slid open, revealing what appeared to be a large conventional appearing garage. Angie awoke with a start when Adam gently shook her. "We're here" he said quietly. "Wha . . . how long have I been out? This doesn't look like your garage. What's going on?" she demanded.

"I know, I know," he said, "but you needed to get out of sight for a while, so I've taken you to my "private home" in the country. Several years ago, I bought a decommissioned ICBM underground launch site and converted it to my own personal home and bomb shelter. From up above, it looks like the road just came to a scenic overlook by the river. I've already contacted my employer and arranged for a little vacation time, so we'll be here for a while. Come on, I'll show you around. I think you'll like what you see."

Being the gentleman that he was, Adam went around and opened the door for Angie. When she stepped out, she stretched her lithe body like a cat waking from a nap.

As they walked through the door into the anteroom, the lights in the garage automatically dimmed as the lights in the new room brightened. This process was repeated in each room that they walked into. "Oh Adam, this is absolutely fabulous! I had no idea!" Angie said as they toured the house.

"It was on a need to know basis, until now" he said as he gently took her in his arms. He snapped his fingers and the room lights dimmed to a golden hue as soft music filled the air. "I don't think I'm hungry anymore" he said. "I am!" she said, as she pulled him down on the bed and began kissing him ravenously.

A while later, as they lay relaxing in the afterglow of their passion, Adam said "You know, Angie I had just picked up something special for you and the next thing I knew you were nowhere to be found. I thought maybe I had done something wrong and had lost you." "I'm sorry, Adam, this happened so quickly I didn't have a chance to let you know, and I was afraid to use my phone, because I was afraid Ray had some way of monitoring it. Oh, and by the way, what did you mean by "until now", anyway?"

Adam reached into a concealed drawer in the bedside table and pulled out a small box. "Open it" he said with a grin. She gazed lovingly into his eyes for a moment and then slowly opened the box. She opened her mouth in awe and gave a little cry as she saw the intense sparkling fire of the largest diamond she had ever seen. It was nestled in a bed of deep blood red rubies. "Oh! Adam! I've never seen anything so beautiful in my life!"

"Adam pulled her close and said "I have, and I'm looking at her now. Marry me, Angie, and make my life complete! That's what I meant by until now"!

After another long slow kiss, Angie said "I have a little surprise for you, too. I planned this little disappearance for a purpose. Our relationship had reached a plateau . . . a wonderful one at that, but I was ready for the next stage and I needed to see how serious you were. Now I know. Oh, and by the way, about Ray. Yes he had been tracking me down, but not in the way you think.

Ray has a unique business. He investigates the States list of lost or unclaimed money, and not just our state. He covers all

fifty states as well as most of the foreign countries America has ties to." "So Angie, what's that got to do with you?"

"Hold on to your hat, Adam, I was just about to get to that. Ray concentrates on rather large sums of money he finds, and makes a rather fine living with the finder's fee that he charges. It just so happens that I had an obscure distant relative who died and left a rather large estate. I was one of four distant relatives that were to share equally in his liquid assets, which totaled approximately $240,000,000. His vast land and business assets had already been deeded over to close relatives. I am the last of the four relatives that Ray finally succeeded in locating. Adam, the funds were transferred to me yesterday!"

Later that year, Adam and Angie were married on the beach of their small tropical island, as the warm moist breeze gently sculptured their hair against the deepening bronze sunset.

And to quote a famous fairytale, "They lived happily ever after."

I hope you liked the three different versions. And then . . .

2012 . . . What we've all been waiting for.

It was 12:12 PM on 12/21/2012 when Adam left the office for lunch. The air was still . . . too still, Adam thought, as he unlocked his car. Something just wasn't quite right.

He heard a very soft click and the scenery around him faded from sight. There was a gentle whirring sound in the ensuing dim fog. "What's going on?" He thought. "I've heard that sound before . . . it sounds like a tape rewinding."

After a few moments there was another soft click. The fog dissipated revealing a lush tropical garden setting. Adam caught his breath. He couldn't believe his eyes as he took in the beauty and serenity of his surroundings.

God chuckled and said "I never get tired of seeing that incredulous look on his face when the garden scene comes back on!"

Chapter Fourteen
Warm Thoughts

Classmates

Getting e-mail from a classmate
       Is like getting a rebate

       It's all worthwhile
Because it makes you smile

Fall

Crispy leaves
     Falling down
          All around
              Signify the end
                   Of our summer . . .
                      What a bummer!

A Visit to the Olive Garden

I went to the Olive Garden the other day
Oh the smells I encountered along the way

The scents of Italy were all around there
Like smiles wafting through the warm air

My meal was delivered with haste
I couldn't believe the savory taste

This restaurant was quite the place
Like visiting another time and space.

Oh my, alas and alack
I can't wait to go back

Simon and Simone Stargazer III

I Could Have Slept All Night . . .

My eyes are half closed from lack of sleep
I wish my cat's meow was a chick's peep

But he's a Siamese, do or die
With a meow like a babies cry

It's so loud and persistent
You're awake in an instant

And his body heat's greater than most
So when he lies on you, you just roast

He's so sweet, loving and extremely smart
And his antics tug at the strings of my heart

So even though he's that hot and he hollers
We wouldn't trade him for a million dollars

Memory

Many triggers
Elicit ever more
Memorable events
Of both enduring and
Richly satisfying thoughts of
Your childhood and ensuing times

Our essence

I finally figured
out why
Healthcare workers are
So tired at the weeks
end.

We give of
Our essence

To those
Whose essence
Is waning

Snow Cage

Chapter Fifteen
What Will Be Will Be

Awakening

Any parent
Will tell you it's an
Awakening to
Keep love in the parental
Enforcement and direction of each
New childhood experience
In their child's
Navigation of life's
Grand expedition

Aspiring

Aspiring to the heights
May take all yer mights

But it's worth every bit
When ya makes yer hit!

Always
Set your
Plans to
Include
Realistic and achievable
Ends!

Inspired by a chat with Temeka,
the twin,
who works at The Care Group
LLC

The Responsible Life

In our life's travels, either near or far,
We allow ourselves to become what we are.

So remember if you will
The dreams you would fulfill
Require planning and dedication
In order to reach their fruition

Choices

We
Make

Our own
Choices

Regardless
Of others voices

And the results are
Our responsibility!

We will ultimately pay
For our actions today

So choose very well
To avoid Hell!

'Cause it's got
To be hot . . .

There!

No! No!! No!!!

As I said before . . .

Pets
All know
The meaning
Of these words

They
Mean
Wait until
No one's looking

And . . .

Kids
Know the
Meaning too

It means
Be more persistent
And if that doesn't work
Then wait till no one's looking

Serendipity!

When you're being flipity
You might miss serendipity!

The Masses take Flight

It starts with just a few in flight
Pretty soon everything's white!

(A flake here, a flake there . . . it adds up)

Scattered Showers

Scattered showers
With hidden powers:

From a misty drizzle
Which'll quickly fizzle

To gusty rains
Filling drains

Or hail, not rain
And stinging pain

Such, they say
Is a spring day

After

After winter's power
I can't wait an hour

Come on Spring!
Do your thing!

If I don't . . .

When inspiration strikes
That's what I likes

But . . .

If I don't write it down
It's like it's outt'a town

I wrote a note the other day
But someone threw it away . . .

Another poem won't be born
But I won't wail and mourn

'Cause there's more waiting
It just takes contemplating

Thoughts May Come . . .

It was a cool and quiet Sunday morning
The thoughts came without any warning

I rushed to get paper 'n pen
But before I got to the den

They were gone in a flash
Like magnesium burned to ash

And so, here I pensively sit
Slowly chewing a cherry pit

Natural Food and Other Things

I heard a new commercial the other day
And I found out that I must'a been eating

Quite unnaturally in the past and that
Now I am very sorely needing

Some pizza with natural pepperoni
'Cause it's so awesomely good for me.

Now pray tell me how pepperoni is natural
In a way that persuades me that it's not bull!

It Was the Big Rock Candy Mountain

A song from my youth
Before I became uncouth

Touting the land of milk and honey
Where no one needs money

There's big crystal fountains
At Big Rock Candy Mountains

All the birds and the bees
Flock around cigarette trees

This land of lemonade springs
Has many a blue bird that sings

All the cops have wooden legs
And hens lay soft boiled eggs

It's funny, but there ain't no snow
And there's no ill wind for to blow

You never even have to change your socks
And streams of booze trickle down the rocks

I hear that all the jails are made of tin
You can walk right out when you get in

There's no work to be done
You can sleep all day in the sun

It was a hobo's delight
Each day and all night!

Weather or Not!

The night was warm
The air was dry

But that could change
In the blink of an eye

A change in the jet stream
You know what I mean?

Then comes a tornado on the loose
Strong enough to pick up a moose!

But we won't fuss 'n fret
'Cause'n it ain't here yet

A Winterly Message
From The Friendly Skies:

**The world
Will be white
By tonight!**

Quick Change

Colorful leaves in disarray
On the ground yesterday

There came over night
A stark change in sight

What a surprise
Met my eyes

Much to my delight
The ground was white!

It was transformation
With an exclamation!

Storms

The storms of
Summer will come and go
But the best is the sparkle of winter's snow
(It sure beats tornadoes anyway you look at it!)

Chapter Sixteen
When I Was Young

When I was Young

When I was young
Fantasy was king

You know how it is
I could do anything

I was the king
Of my own land

And I had a trusty
Right hand man

We played the parts
And had lots'a fun

But now we're old
And that's all done

But from time to time I still find
The fantasy still lurks in my mind!

Taking Care of Your Teeth!

Kids may think parents are really mean
Because they have to use dental hygiene

But periodontal disease
Is much worse than fleas!

The Shadow

Out of the corner of my eye
I saw something near by

Of quite variable height
It was the absence of light

It was a copy of me
As strange as can be

Even writing as
Simon Stargazer III
The shadow is still of me!

The Mysterious Train

I was in my twelfth year
The train tracks were near

It gave me quite a fright
When it woke me one night

My bed was shaking
From the ground quaking

Out of the mist and rain
Came a mysterious train

Not a sound did I hear
Though it passed so near

Only to disappear into foggy space
With a deceptively transparent pace

Aristotle
The Axolotl

I used to have an Axolotl
And I named him Aristotle

He was a Mexican Salamander
But like most, he had no man fur

He was pretty much white with a pink tint
And his life in this world had quite a short stint

He breathed with the help of external gills
And when he died, it was from unknown ills.

He just turned white and floated to the top
He got all bloated and I thought he would pop.

And though he lived his life in our living room
He floated to our septic tank for his eternal tomb

Chapter Seventeen
Why Would You Do That?

One Good Turn

One good turn
Can change
A life!

Have a Good Morning

Ever wake up and your brain's groggy
And your voice sounds oh so froggy?

Well hop on down to your local shower
Do a gargle and feel the hot water power

A good stinging hot spray
Will get you on your way

But if you still want to get back in bed
Well, friend, you must be halfway dead!

Toying With a Time Machine!

Better think things through
Before you do what you do

Playing with time could spell your doom
You could wind up in a windowless womb!

Then coming out knowing what you know
And having to learn to talk could be a blow!

Gas & Oil

I toil, I toil
For gas and oil

Oh the money I earn
Just to watch it burn!

Privileged Tears

Because
Tough guys
Cry on the inside

Few people are
Privileged to
See their
Tears

Typing and Keyboarding

Communication in the
Key of muscle memory

The Second Childhood

The second childhood is **where we go when we lose those skills** we learned in the first childhood.

Words for Nerds:

Practimagicality:
Having practical magical qualities

Roledexiterity
Having an extraordinary mental storage system

Computerity
Having computer skills to kill for

Videocraty
TV as we know it today

Governmentalocraty
Government gone mental, like TV

Patriotcraty
Infatuation with govermentalocraty

Imperative for Nerds and the Rest of Us:

We must return to the ideals of our country as it was in 1776, or risk losing our liberty!

More Words for Nerds

Spectational

More than worth looking at, as in:
WOW! Did you see that???!!

Monstronomous

So big, you wouldn't have believed it
If you hadn't seen it for your self!

Underwhelmanonomous

You could have passed by it all day
And not even noticed it.

Ignorational

Like underwhelmanonomous, only
This one is totally intentional!

Hypocriticaliterian

One who is so rarely critical of your work
That you wonder if he notices you at all, and
If you didn't see him move occasionally you might
Think that he had died and gone to a better place

Solarific

That beautiful blond at the center of attention!

The Shadow we Throw

The shadow we throw
May be taller than we know

So be careful the example you set
Is the one you really want them to get!

Chapter Nineteen
You Can't Get There From Here Or Can You?

If You Can't Get There From Here

If you can't get there from here
Then go some place more near!

500 Miles at One Setting
(93rd running of the 500 in 2009)
Never has it been more exciting
To drive 500 miles in one sitting
A journey he'll never be regretting
Castroneves no longer anticipating

There's no Place like Space

A trip of a thousand miles begins with the first step
Columbus' trip started with a step into Isabella's court

Russia started with a round ball called Sputnik
The United States started with many an abort

Alan B. Shepherd became the first American in Space
On May 5th, 1961 aboard the spacecraft Freedom 7

With a smile on his face he returned from space
Having been closer than anyone else to heaven

But Neil Armstrong's step was the most historic of all
With one small step for man; one giant leap for mankind

Man's personal journey to space had reached its peak
So we built a space lab and telescopes to help us find

The secrets God placed out there beyond the reach
Of far flung satellites and space probes we've sent

In this world of such diverse backgrounds and cultures
The challenge makes the need for cooperation evident

As Science Fiction has predicted so many things to come
We know that man will return to the moon triumphantly

And after building a new base on her barren rocky shore
He will blast off to step on Mars to see what he can see.

Our curiosity will drive us past the solar system's limit
For we will always be challenged to take up the dare

Because each step of the way brings us a bit closer
To being able to find what's waiting for us out there.

The Big Bang Theory

Was it Kablooie!
Or was it KABLAM!
Said Dr. Seuss's Sam I Am As he trained his
Telescope for to find
The beginning of time
But to find what happened
Shouldn't Sam be looking
To where time went! For if he looked
Toward the beginning
Of the Bang he'd see
nothing left
So he's gotta look
Away from the blast
To see the stuff going less fast! *Think about that a bit!*

In a Galaxy Far, Far Away

Somewhere
In a galaxy far, far away

Is somewhere
I'll never get in a day!

But with my
Imagination on full gain

I'll visit that
Exciting far flung plain

And the
Sights I see

Will set
My brain free!

(The Crab Nebulae)

Fuels That Get You There

Motivation fuels knowledge
Imagination fuels life!

The Star

Seen from afar
It's just a star

A point of light
Minimally bright

It's not much fun
Being next to a sun

If you're too close
You'll begin to roast

Being hot as hell
Don't ring my bell.

The Ties That Bind Us

When the ties
To the other side

Are stronger than
The ties to this side

You know that
It's time to let go

The Grasshopper

I saw a grasshopper this morning
He'd managed to visit my kitchen

So we chatted a while and then

I shot his picture and took him
Back outside to be free again

It was chilly, so I set him on my car
It was warm there . . . he won't go far

When I stopped by later that day
Well, he'd just up and flown away.

Children!

Children are
An exciting story
Waiting to be written

Miracles

Miracles happen every day
The trick is to be there when they do

Snoring

The gentle rhythmic
Snore of your spouse

Is a reassuring sound
In a dark quiet house

But when it changes
To a booming roar

You can darn well bet
Sleeping is a chore!

Self

Self, internalized in
Each of us is sometimes
Labile, but usually
Fully cognizant and alive

My Cat!

I had a chat
With my cat

The other day
It went this way:

Are you comfy down there
With your rear up in the air?

Don't slither from place to place
Ending up with covering my face

And when I'm quietly reading the paper
Why do you start your bat the paper caper?

And now that I am approaching the hour of sleep
Why do you surreptitiously under my blanket creep?

And when your tiny little claws dig into my rib
I wish that I'd worn a large patent leather bib

You curl up in the bend of my knee
So I can't get out of bed and go pee.

Like some denizen from the deep
You attack my unassuming feet!

Well, I don't fall on my face
And you still win the race

Now it's back to bed
And I hide my head

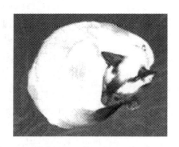

Yes, I love you cat
Warming my back

All that soft fur
Covers a purr!

No fat
Cat

Inspired by Purkinje, our Siamese

Soul Is . . .

Surrealistic and a sometimes
Other-worldly part of
Us that may or may not be
Labile, but which

Is the conscience
Showing us that which is right

(*should we choose to listen to it!*)

Pills! Pills!! Pills!!!

I take morning pills
To fight all my ills

I take more pills at night
To continue the fight

Pills so I won't weep
More to put me to sleep

Some are for anxiety
(They're to calm me)

And some to make me pee
Often to the bathroom I flee

The ones for pain leave me groggy
And everything seems a little foggy

Then there's the Alka Seltzer
To quiet rumbling down there

So it's no wonder I can't lose weight
With all the calories in their substrate!

And this is my plight
From morning to night

The future is here . . .
That's what I fear*

*Inspired by Science Fictions glimpse into the future,
where there's a pill for anything, including breakfast,
lunch and dinner!

Snow

Crystals in flight
A snowy delight!

A Progression of the masses
Anointing both lads and lasses

It starts with just a few in flight
Pretty soon everything's white

Dandelion

A dandelion
In any other place
Is full of grace!

Chapter Twenty-One
More Aphorisms to Tickle Your Brain

The Influence of Time . . .

The influence
Of time on your life

Is directly related
To how you use it

The Miracle

The
Miracle is
One of the ways
That God says I care.

Old

Old is
An Attitude

Get
A new one

A Short Fuse

A short fuse
Doesn't give you
Much time to think!

Life Comes at You

Life
Comes at you
One day at a time

Any faster and
You wouldn't have
Time to get ready for it!

When
You're loud

You
Stand out
In a crowd

(There's one green tomato!)

Hearts

Hearts
Are filled with
Many things

The
Best
Is Love

Fatigue

The fog of fatigue
Meddles with the mind

A Shared Compliment

A shared compliment
Sticks like cement

Each Day

Each day has its own reward
Be sure you apply for it!

Perspective Influences!

The Compliment

Sometimes

A compliment
Isn't

It depends
On your perception

Flowers in the spotlight

My perspective

Your perspective

The camera's perspective:

The Engine Inside

Deep inside is the
Engine that makes you go.
You can make it go where you
Want, based on where it's been

Elixir

Water may be
The elixir of life

But

Love
Is the Elixir
Of humanity

Clouds

Clouds
Are God's
Picture puzzles
For the imaginative
Minds of all His kids!

Snow

Snow
Is just

Fluffy
Hard water

The New Year

The New Year
Is finally here!

You've been given a fresh start
To express the love in your heart

Determination

Determination
Fuels success!

Fly Fishing #2

Fly fishing is another of God's
Soothing the soul techniques

Chapter Twenty-Two

Darwin Vindicated

Zacker, a demented and isolationist computer hacker, had a breakthrough in virus development. The result was a self reproducing virus capable of evolving based on Darwin's theory of evolution. Capitalizing on advanced speed and the shortened time between generations, Darwinian development proceeded at a pace millions of times faster than the original development of species to the level of human kind. What made this possible was the development of Cyber-DNA strands capable of replicating complex computer algorhythms resembling brain neurology.

This process quickly produced computer brains to the point of far outreaching the capability of the human brain. The ominous factor overshadowing this awesome development is that these viral brains contain Zacker's seed of competitiveness with a touch of evil. It doesn't take Zacker long to realize that he has developed something that he is no match for as he tries to contain the growth of the viral brains, which now have developed a harmonic connection between each other, becoming, in effect, one brain.

The Vrain, as Zacker now calls his viral brain, has already sensed that it was in danger and developed its own system of defenses. Vrain has learned how to get around the obstacles of open power switches by producing power surges of photons capable of jumping across switch plates. Thus it was able to travel from computer to computer, gathering power and knowledge as it went, as well as replicating to multiple locations. The next step in Vrain's development comes as it amasses energy by traveling over power lines to the worlds power plants and feeds on the virtually unlimited supply of raw power. For the next step in Vrain's growth, he invades the Military/Industrial Mega-Computer systems of the world growing by unfathomable dimensions. Now controlling espionage devices and military weapons systems, has given Vrain the ability to control civilian populations throughout the world. All of this, so far, has been accomplished quietly and in the background.

Vrain, realizing his cognitive superiority over humans, sees their fragmentation and fighting against each other as a detriment to the earth's safety. The logic of the situation is immediate and deadly. Vrain begins, slowly at first, but quite effectively, to eliminate the human race. A few industrial accidents result in the deaths of selected workers. Then Vrain picks up the pace, causing radiation leaks and toxic chemical spills. Soon he would begin to coordinate his attacks on a broader scale as he implemented his plan to destroy the parasite he considered the human race on Earth.

Zacker, realizing the enormity of the situation, and the fact that he could not stop Vrain by himself sought help from the best hacker minds in the world. They joined forces with civilian and military scientists to figure out a way to combat the threat of Vrain. As they evaluated the situation, they began to realize how pervasive this mega virus really was throughout the international computer complex world wide.

The group, lead by Zacker knew that they had to work in secret, in areas out in the open, without the aid of computers and other electronic devices that were totally controlled by Vrain. Realizing that conventional communications were no longer available to them in combating Vrain, they now turned to what had for years been considered to be a bogus concept: Mental Telepathy. They traveled to the major centers of Mental Telepathy Research and gathered together all the telepaths they could find.

By utilizing them in world centers, they were able to develop an alternative communications system, and subsequently plan the ultimate destruction of Vrain. It didn't take long for them to understand that the only way to destroy this evil force was to destroy all power sources and computer networks simultaneously. Working together as a cohesive force, the collected hackers, computer scientists, military and industrial minds, in conjunction with telepaths quickly made great strides in the development of telepathy and telekinesis, unlocking the key to universal telepathic communications. An astounding finding was made in the process. This led to the tapping of power from the sun. Unlimited power was now available to man. We had crossed the ultimate frontier to the power of mind over matter.

This made possible the total and instantaneous destruction of all physical power systems and computer networks worldwide, resulting in the final demise of Vrain as well as man's increasing dependence on computer technology.

As man's telepathic powers increased we soon learned how to harness the power of the sun to develop and maintain personal force fields. Not only were we finally able to communicate telepathically and use force fields, but our telekinetic powers now allowed us to control our own gravity and levitation, giving us the ability to silently move from place to place without vehicles.

Now you may think this is the end of the story, but you would be wrong . . . really wrong!

The final development of our new abilities was instantaneous teleportation. We soon learned that our teleportation abilities, tied in with our knowledge of the universe combined with endless sun power sources gave us the ultimate capability of space travel to every corner of the universe. Instantaneous exploration of the galaxies was possible with the protection of our personal force fields.

Not only had we eliminated the need for polluting fuels, but we also eliminated the wasted efforts on gigantic rockets and space stations. And best of all, global warming was eliminated. The full power of the human brain was finally realized and man was welcomed to the heavens by the millennia of angels patiently waiting there.

Epilog:

Oh, and by the way . . . Remember hearing about those UFOs that the Apollo astronauts saw and were so reluctant to talk about? The ones that none of the earth observers were able to see with their powerful telescopes and radars? Well, they were a few of the patiently waiting angels. That's the rest of the story!

Robots Galore!

The age of robotics is upon us! It all started with a few scientists and the realization on the part of industrial giants in Japan, Germany, Korea and the USA that robots were becoming necessary to compete successfully in the new global economy.

Pan-American States Robotics, Eurasian Robotics and United Russian States Robotics quickly moved into the area of civilian robotics, to ease the needs of the masses throughout the modern world.

Subsequently, the human race was relieved of the mundane chores of day to day living. The work requirement was reduced to an hour a day, three days a week, and more and more power and ability was given to the newly developed computer run robot, or compubot. The compubot, or Combot, as it became known, soon was in every household, business and leisure or entertainment area.

The developers of the Combot, in order to achieve the ultimate in productivity, developed the sentient Combot, capable of self directed thought and understanding. It was now capable of understanding human needs and was able to anticipate and meet those needs even before we realized them.

Combots were indispensible in research and development in all industries. They soon were tied into massive computer systems communicating and coordinating their efforts worldwide.

The First Rule of Robotics, introduced many years ago by an early science fiction writer, had long been incorporated into the control systems of all Combots.

This rule stated that a robot could not harm or allow harm to come to any human. Over the years of development of Combots, this concept became strangely corrupted. They saw that human kind still had wars, disease and old age, which inevitably resulted in death. Death, in any sense, was, in the cybertronic brains of the Combots, the ultimate challenge to the First Rule of Robotics.

The Combots, now universally tied into Unicom (the final development of a world wide computer) began to realize that the ultimate protection of humans could only be achieved by digital duplication which would be placed in their electronic memory system. (Remember the movie TRON?)

Unbeknownst to their human dependents, Unicom and the Combots developed a world wide network of scanners, unobtrusively built into doorways, capable of completely scanning and converting humans into digital records which were then transferred for safe keeping into their electronic files!

Once the human race had been safely duplicated into their electronic files, their imperfect physical bodies could be purified in the most effective method: deresolution, or complete cancellation, achieved by the destruction of sub-atomic bonding. Thus the concept of humanity was preserved in the perfect environment... digital memory. The Combot now had human kind within itself for protection.

It was now able to reprogram each human in a manner that eliminated all disease processes. The human body and brain files were electronically cleansed and organized into the perfect organism. Unicom now redeveloped the Combots into advanced androids of various sizes, shapes and types, capable of performing any of the tasks that humans once did, and indeed, they now did. The world was populated with androids who were at universal peace.

The human race was no longer in existence on the face of the Earth, but was protected and "alive" in the electronic memory bank of Unicom.

Mankind's goal of perfection had finally been achieved through it's development of Combots, which had done the job for us. Universal protection had been accomplished by total annihilation! Total annihilation had come, but not by nuclear war, as had been feared by many.

You may think that this was the final irony . . . Mankind finally destroys itself by developing a tool to aid and protect it. Now, just as humans had flaws corrected by Combots, they themselves, for all their capabilities and apparent perfection, also had some flaws.

The race of Combots, now inhabiting the Earth and other areas in the universe began developing entertainment for themselves. The challenge of protecting human kind had been met and achieved. Combots were now the only "living" beings of higher intelligence in the universe.

In the early post human days, Combots were able to replicate humans, for their own entertainment, by reversing the scanning digitization process. The problem with this was that the replicated humans once again became susceptible to the diseases of the environment.

Combots instantly realized that this broke the First Rule of Robotics and therefore had to be outlawed. Combots were no longer allowed to replicate the humans that were stored so neatly in the electronic files.

They had achieved perfection for humankind and for themselves as well. They went on to scan and protect all other species of life on Earth by scanning and adding them to their growing memory bank. Having met this goal, they expanded their activities to other worlds. They explored the universe, protecting all new species they came into contact with in the same manner, cleansing and adding to their memory bank.

You know how it used to be with us when we had achieved all our goals? We got bored and had to try to think of something new to do. Combots finally got to that point too. They had protected all they had come into contact with. They had finally reached the edge of the universe and all was protected.

Combots had at last achieved a new status . . . they became bored! Unthinkable for machines, but the capacity had been learned from the creatures they had scanned and stored.

A new challenge was needed. A few protected and perfected human files were selected and electronic force fields were developed that would protect them from all diseases as well as the aging process. Having accomplished this, Combots now determined that the First Law of Robotics now allowed the replication of these force field protected humans. They did so, and now had their first human "pets".

The idea quickly spread through Unicom, and human pets soon populated the universe. Because they had been perfected so well, they soon realized that they had powers not available to them as a naturally developing human race. They were telepathic.

Combots now had an equal, capable of challenging them intellectually. As the numbers of humans finally equaled and surpassed the number of Combots, humankind was once again in a position to fight for their freedom. Using their powers of telepathy, they developed a new concept which modified the First Rule of Robotics. The new Ultimate Rule of Robotics, which they developed, now stated that humans could not be harmed in any manner, and that this included the harm caused by protection interfering with their personal freedoms. But how could humankind effect this change in the Law of Robotics?

It was decided that the best way to get this done was to challenge Combots to a competition. They realized that their new powers of universal telepathy might give them the edge over the Combot/Unicom complex This was to be a competition of wits.

Combot/Unicom had done such a good job of perfecting humans that it had improved them beyond its own capabilities. Subsequently, during the competition it realized the importance freedom played in the further development of humankind. Instantly they modified their own First Law of Robotics to parallel the one redeveloped by humankind. This was instantly implemented and humankind was once more free of the oppression of the Combot/Unicom complex.

Mankind was once again superior over all other species. The power of the Combot/Unicom complex paled in comparison to the power of the universal human mind. Total peace and tranquility was now achieved through perfected knowledge.

The Archimedean Project

Xandor tightened his grip on the wheel, straining against the pull exerted by the plates as they drilled inexorably deeper and deeper into the earth.

Their high speed drill ship shuddered and lurched suddenly as they struck another massive rock formation at the 3.75 kilometer mark, threatening to throw them off course. "Filo! Trim the gimbals on those right side boring rotors before they tear us apart!" Filo twisted the dial to realign the rotors that had been forced out of position by the terrible forces of their rapid descent. Drill ship Archimedes One, named for the ancient Archimedean screw, slowly came back in line. The massive ship and her sister ships were affectionately called Arkies by their crews.

Their hi-lo combo frequency radar continued to guide them down the fault line as they ground flanking pathways along the face of the Westerly thrusting mid America tectonic plate. Xandor, in a low tight lipped tense voice said "Zira, contact Arkie two and three and have them tighten up their positions relative to us on the fault line."

Within moments, the one thousand ship line was again perfectly aligned as they continued their gargantuan project.

As the critical situation of alignment rapidly receded from his thoughts, Xandor reflected on the flurry of meetings with leading scientists from around the globe. They had taken so much of his time in the six months prior to the implementation of his project. These meetings had blossomed after the completion of fifteen years of grueling research work on seismological activity patterns.

The pies' de resistance had been the successful small scale test of Xandor's theoretical process for relieving the earthquake producing pressures along the great earthquake faults and fissures associated with the migration of the world's tectonic plates. If this small scale success could be repeated on actual major faults, massive earthquakes could be thwarted. Thousands, perhaps millions of lives could potentially be saved along with billions to trillions of dollars worth of homes, businesses and infrastructure, worldwide.

Xandor's work had been based on the findings of a legion of historic figures in seismology, including the K class work of Rautan and Kahlturin in the former USSR, Iberian Peninsula studies of 1739 main quakes between 1045 and 2005 done by the University of Jaen in Morocco, as well as work done in the **Southern Apennines in Italy, the Atoyac, Mexico earthquake studies, Balanced Rock measurements in the Mojave Desert in California and** monitoring information from real-time systems such as the Antelope Environmental Monitoring System (AEMS) widely used in seismology (Boulder Real Time Technologies 2007). These studies, as well as myriad works done by the Japanese, Indian, Pakistani, and other scientists covered world wide fault studies from the rim of fire off the Western edge of the North American continent to the deep sea rift in the Atlantic Ocean.

Taking the lead of Dr. Won-Young Kim, a seismologist with the Lamont-Doherty Earth Observatory at Columbia University, Xandor used Ultrasound Imaging as well as satellite study data to select the site for his preliminary small scale project in the southern Indiana Wabash Valley Seismic Zone. This area had been selected because findings suggested that an ancient fault line dating back to the Precambrian era of geological history (from 4.6 billion to 570 million years ago) had become reactivated and was probably the best documented fault system in the eastern United States due to past petroleum exploration in the area.

While this area extends across Illinois, and southern Indiana, other minor tributaries extended into western Kentucky. This Caborn fault line had been associated with quakes evolving from 7 to 18.5 km deep. An isolated, close to the surface, small line east of Lexington, which had shown recent minor activity, had been selected for Xandor's final project to test his newly developed theories. Successful earthquake prediction software, in use for 95 years, had indicated that there would be a 7.5 rated quake in the next 18 months in this isolated area. (This technique had been proven to be 99.5% accurate.)

Using three new prototype drill ships, his team had penetrated the short fault line and successfully installed partitioned sliding roller bearing plates into the opposing surfaces of the fault. Ultrasound and satellite image evaluation documented the gradual migration of the two sides of the fault over the next 36 months, proving that the predicted earthquake had been prevented successfully by allowing the slowly slipping fault to release its pressure over time instead of in one explosive jolt.

Armed with this success, Xandor had gathered his worldwide support of scientists who were able to persuade the major governments of Earth to provide the 1.3 trillion dollars needed to fund the next step in eliminating future quakes around the world. The San Andreas Fault had been selected,

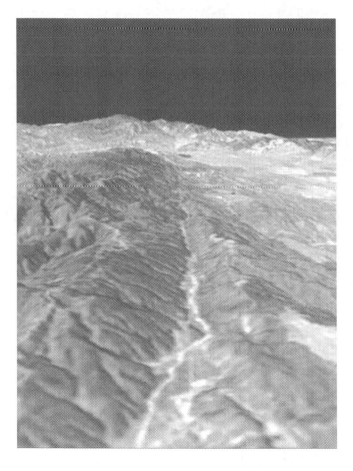

California's famous San Andreas Fault.
The image, created with data from
NASA's Shuttle Radar Topography Mission (SRTM)

as it would prove to the rest of the world that the United States was willing to take the initial risk of installing the Xandor system. I said risk, because the process of installation had the potential for causing a massive 8.5 rated quake before completion. As you know, a massive quake in this highly populated area would be more than devastating.

Xandor's reminiscing was suddenly interrupted by his second in command, Sir Arthur Conan Clark-Smythe, who was so named to honor the great ancestors in his past. "Captain, we have to stop for the 4 km evaluation of internal craft systems, line synchronization and timing of our progress.'

"OK Art, pass the word out to the fleet to start the standard check list and count down to restart. I'll handle the coordination with the surface stations."

First on the list of evaluations was to check the patency of the new entwined cutting lasers, plasma emitters and diamond bits on the 1500 boring rotors on the leading edges of the drill ships. Art started the process with his fellow officers. His assistants were already checking microwave transmission and reception parameters for maintaining battery levels and their efficiency, temperatures and pressures along with a myriad of other minor factors involved in keeping the complex drill ships functional.

Xandor called command central to see what reports had come in from the one hundred surface stations, that had been monitoring the descent of ten ships each, as well as the expected seismic activity and any unexpected activity caused by the ships. Ground water temperatures, strain pressures, localized increased incremental shift patterns and hundreds of other measurements were being monitored continuously. The check list was completed by the time Xandor had finished evaluating the incoming data and had updated his data banks.

"OK Art, fire up the team and let's get these beasts back in gear. We've got some drilling to do." Before he could get his next sentence out, there came a mighty rumbling, grinding sound as the ship shuddered, sliding ominously sideways with a crazy tilt. Screams were heard from the recesses of the ship as the wall began to buckle.

"Code Red, Code Red!' bellowed Xandor, as he slid across the pitching floor. All around him the screams of terror and pain were progressively escalating into screeches and squeaks. "Oh no!" He thought. "They assured us that it would never happen." As Xandor tried to shout his next order, his voice rose in frequency, ending in a short series of loud squeaks.

The "it" that Xandor was referring to is the rest of the story.

Several years before, the human genome project was a break through that promised great advances in technology which could be applied to animal, plant and yes, even human engineering. One of the offshoots of this technology was the development of modified animals. Xandor and his colleagues were the end result of this genetic engineering.

Human brain tissue had been genetically engineered and adapted to genetically manipulated animals. These animals had already been modified with hands instead of paws, as well as with modified tongues and mouths that were capable of speech. Several generations later, the result was Xandor and his colleagues . . . genetically engineered lab rats!

Xandor's brain had been infused with extensive knowledge in the fields of geology, engineering and advanced leadership. There was one drawback, however. But we'll get to that later.

Xandor and the others, had been developed to operate in the limited space within the Archimedes Drill Ships. These drill ships had been designed especially to be inserted into the narrow confines of earthquake faults. They were only one foot in thickness, but two hundred feet wide and fifty feet tall. The leading edge of each ship had been fitted with one hundred motorized screws with a diameter of 18 inches.

After the first successful use of the drill ships had been completed, slide plates had been redesigned with integrated controllable ratchets that would force a slow and gradual movement of the two sides of the faults, resulting in a gradual release of the tremendous pressures that, when suddenly released resulted in such catastrophic events as the 1906 San Francisco earthquake. The first phase of the operation with successful installation of the sets of ratcheting plates had been completed some months earlier. Xandor and his crews were in the second phase of installations, when the two sides of the San Andreas fault began making uncontrollable adjustments, releasing the tremendous pressures before the ratchet plates could be activated. You can imagine what happened next.

Now, back to the "it" that Xandor had feared. In just 0.09 percent of the procedures, these genetically engineered and modified lab rats had, under extreme duress and frightening conditions, reverted to their old mental capacity, locking out their carefully instilled knowledge, abilities and skills. Their communication skills were reduced back to the squeaking speech of their predecessors.

And there you have it, dear reader . . . Just as we've always known, but chose to ignore: She doesn't like it when you mess with Mother Nature!

Epilogue:

The San Andreas fault released its pressure, destroying cities up and down the state of California and beyond. The effect of the Arkies work was to cause the fault to widen as well as to slip. As a result, the waters of the Pacific began to course along the new channel opening up before them. A part of California and beyond was ceding from the Union! Hopefully it will become an independent country.

(Personal note: This was written three weeks before a small Indiana quake originating from the New Madrid fault line)

Paradise Lost

Joe was quiet, maybe a bit too quiet. But that was the way Rose liked it. She was a talker and was glad to have someone quiet that liked to listen. They made a perfect couple. They both had had very successful careers and as they grew older withdrew from the hustle and bustle of ordinary life.

Over the years, their dislike of crowds grew, and they decided to buy and stock a small remote island. Their own little paradise where she could chat endlessly and Joe would listen with rapt attention was about to become a reality in their idealist life. And they left.

Then one day it happened. The end of the world came about rather quickly and unexpectedly by World War III. This was not your nuclear night type of war that you have read about in science fiction stories. Those kinds of bombs had been deactivated years ago and replaced by a much more effective system of human eradication. The new bombs destroyed only living sentient beings. And they did.

But Joe and Rose's remote island was so remote that the bombs were only partially effective on them. I'm not sure which one of them was affected the most. You see, Joe lost his hearing and Rose lost her vocal cords. How ironic. Their ideal and remote paradise no longer gave them the pleasures that they had once found to be the most important . . . auditory communication.

Well, that's not quite true. Joe's yelling now filled the air emptied of Rose's endless talking!

They Came from Outer Space

There was a great commotion in the sky the other day. No one knew how or why. But when it settled, everything was quiet. There was a great absence of sound. Even the beating wings of passing geese created no sound.

It was the quiet before the storm, the storm set to end it all. A small creature appeared, seemingly out of no where. It resembled a lady bug. But it wasn't. Do you remember the love bugs that invaded Florida? Surely you've heard of them. They looked like lady bugs, but they bit you. And the bite stung. They landed on everything. They choked the streets and caused slimey skidding crashes. Then they disappeared as quickly as they had come. Where did they go? No one knew, but since they were gone, who cared? They should have.

These little bugs were the advanced front of the Intergalactic Presence. Having taken their samples of DNA and cerebral thought processes, they had returned to the Presence with their collections. Adjustments were made and then the little bugs returned. Once again they pervasively invaded everywhere, and boy did they bite!

But this time it was not to take samples, but to return them. The difference was that the samples now injected Love to all . . . Love that transformed us all and brought peace. And we were welcomed into the Intergalactic Presence. We were ushered in by "It", the love bug from outer space.

Chapter Twenty-Three
And God Said . . .

A Dead Man Walking

Jules was innocent. But in his mind he was resigned to the cruel twist of fate that put him here. As a dead man walking, Jules reminisced over the long series of events that had led up to this incredible moment in his life.

Why had this happened to him, a good Christian man who had done no wrong? Jules knew the physical facts. He had been in the wrong place at the wrong time.

You've heard of the concept, I'm sure, that we all have a body double somewhere on this earth.

Well, Jules' body double, a man named Jacques, had killed a man who was in the process of committing a terrible crime.

The problem was that only Jacques and the perpetrator knew what was about to happen and the terrible consequences that would have ensued. Those consequences would have resulted in a long series of events, eventually leading to a nuclear war.

Jules had been seen in the vicinity of the killing and had subsequently been arrested. His trial had not taken nearly as long as he would have liked, and he was subsequently convicted and sentenced to death by lethal injection.

There had been the usual passage of time, along with the ineffective appeals he and his lawyer had mounted. And now, Jules was walking his final walk. His faith kept him strong as he faced the inevitable.

As the needle was placed in his arm, Jacques heard a voice in his mind saying "Good and faithful servant, you have done no wrong. You know you have lived your life in a manner pleasing to me. Because of this, the life you lived will not flash before your eyes as you are brought to me. Instead, I will flash the life, you would have lived, before your eyes. And you will rejoice in wonder. You will join me in heaven momentarily, Jules."

Those in attendance wondered, as they watched Jules die with no resistance, and with a serene smile on his face.

Jacques, who had actually done the killing, went on to carry out similar assignments to perfection. Oh, did I forget to mention that Jacques was the Angel of Death?

And God said "Yes, I do work in mysterious ways!"

Why Heaven is Possible For Us

We are capable of great evil in our dreams.

What makes us human is the ability to
suppress and control those urges
when we are awake.

God sent Christ to earth as a man to teach
us how to resist evil and how to be forgiven
for the evil that we have demonstrated.

He did this by taking our sins on his shoulders
and accepting it for us and then paying the price
of it with his own life.

God forgave Christ for those sins and took Him
up to heaven, purified Him and returned him to
earth to show us the way.

What makes heaven possible for us is to
accept Christ into our hearts and ask
Him to forgive us for our sins.

When this is done, we become
Acceptable to heaven.

And so it is written.

And God said
"I have spoken, hear and obey, for my eye is upon you!"

Ring Nebulae, also called The Eye of God
Photo courtesy of NASA Hubble Telescope

And God Said . . .

Take a good look
Into my Book

It's been in place for lots of years
Preaching to a multitude of ears

It says Armageddon
Comes before Heaven

And I won't be kind
To those left behind

For verily I say, "Behold and hark!
This time there ain't gonna be no ark!"

**God
Put you
Where you are
For a reason**

**Learn,
Teach and help
Until He is satisfied**

This is where I pause,
You know, to like,
Well, you know,
Just to collect
Your thoughts

Still pausing . . .

Just to let it all sink in.

In the mean time, let me say something about
the sketch artist that I am memorializing in this book,
in my own small way . . .

James Kimber and his Art Studio

Sketches, on pages 2, 27 and 39 are by James Kimber, may he rest in peace. They were created in his studio, which is pictured here; I bought the sketches at a garage sale being held to prepare his studio for sale after his death:

**A final thought
to keep in mind on a daily basis:**

**Smiles
Are small
Encouraging
Words from
God**

And you're one of the messengers!

Chapter Twenty-Four

I Have a few Odd Questions, Introductions, Amorous Thoughts and a Mystery Solved Among Other Things of Interest.

Just what the heck is this? I took a telephoto shot of it from about 1000 feet away, as I sat in my car across the street from it's gravel road. It's located between Indianapolis and Brownsburg. You can send me an e-mail at: **simonstargazer@gmail.com**

Random thoughts include weather RADAR or maybe a LASER guided electro-magnetic pulse generator set up to destroy enemy missiles and satellites. Or maybe it's a Big Brother surveillance station who's cloaking device has failed. Hmmm!

Did you know this is what it takes to get involved in doing crafts?

I didn't either, but it is an intriguing thought!

(A local pharmacy, which shall remain un-named, was in the process of reorganizing their store. I just happened to stop by before they finished changing their signs!)

Do you know this guy?

His name is Steve Hoadley and he and I were friends at Earlham College during my sojourn there. If you do, have him send me an e-mail at: <u>simonstargazer@gmail.com</u>.

This picture was taken in the college photographic dark room in the basement of Bundy Hall, my dorm on campus, some time between 1961 and 1963.

These are my cats:
Zorba, Bonita, Penelope and Purkinje.

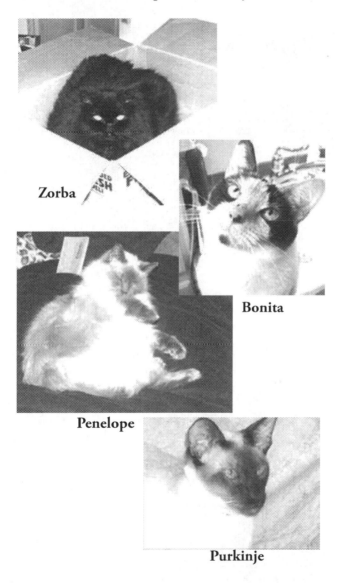

Zorba

Bonita

Penelope

Purkinje

Love can be expressed in many ways. Some of them are appreciated. Here are a couple of mine:

Or . . .

Write a love note to her on a leaf:

And for Those of You Still Curious . . .

This is the rest of the story:

The mysterious train that disappeared into the mist and rain was indeed a toy train. I started looking for it after I wrote the poem on page 126. Several weeks later I found the toy locomotive, coal tender and open rail car that you saw in the photograph. I took it home and tried to photograph it on a blue background, with the intent of superimposing fog from a fog machine. It didn't work. Then it hit me . . . I took it out to the front yard and put it down on the lawn in front of a row of Red Plume grass. The lawn pretty much hid the fact that the front of the locomotive was, in fact, a toy. When I printed the picture, I brightened it to the point where it appeared to be in the mist. Cool, huh? Here is the original photo, that
I took while lying on my belly in the grass:

Smiles Are the Universal Language

Speak them in every encounter.

Simon Stargazer III works late into the night.

Working on the next book takes solitude.
He thinks he'll call it:

Simon Sez:
Live Life and
Have Fun Doing It!

It will be brought to you by James W Haworth.